Terri Peel Bechtold

Momisms:
Life Lessons from a Cool Mom

Momisms: Life Lessons from a Cool Mom

Library of Congress Control Number: 2023910025

ISBN:

979-8-9884366-0-7 (hardcover)
979-8-9884366-1-4 (paperback)

Published by K & T Infinity Publishing Company LLC
Printed in the United States of America
10 9 8 7 6 5 4 3 2

For other books by author Terri Peel Bechtold visit
TerriPeelBechtold.com

To my two greatest achievements,
my two beautiful daughters,
you are my life, purpose, and inspiration.
And to my amazing husband,
always remember and never forget...

I love you For Infinity and Beyond!

MOMISMS... simple sayings... powerful meanings. We all have them, right? Pithy phrases cool moms say to our children when we want to teach them valuable life lessons to guide them through this journey called... life. Momisms help prepare our children to face and conquer life's challenges, and maybe, just maybe, get ahead of the trials and tribulations we know are in their future, so that they can thoroughly experience all of the life we have given to them. Momisms remind our children of the importance of virtues and values, encourage them to be true to themselves, inspire them to strive to reach their fullest potential, and ingrain in them a sense of self-worth and beauty.

Encourage your children to look in the mirror while they prepare for the day ahead and have a great conversation with themselves. Ask them to take a moment to think and talk about the day ahead. To say whatever they want...to think whatever they want... they are the only ones talking...and, hopefully, they are listening! Tell them to always remember and never forget...every second is what you make of it. Every minute is what you make of it. Every hour is what you make of it. Every day is what you make of it. Urge them to look at their reflection in the mirror, really look at themselves, and ask, "What do I want to make of this day?" "What do I want to accomplish?" "What challenges do I need to be ready to tackle?" Remind them to keep their Impowerment app on and ready (more about this Impowerment app after all the Momisms), and then jump right into their day and make it awesome! But if they ever find that they need strength, encouragement, patience, or resilience during any second, minute, or hour of their day, let a Momism come to their rescue and guide them through it! Remind them that life is what you make of it...make it fabulous! And know that these life lessons are not just for our children. They may help you and all the other cool moms and dads through your amazing journey...life's journey! Make yours fabulous, too!

But truth be told, life sometimes makes it very challenging to stay on the right course of thinking, believing, and simply being. Some days this cool mom needs to crack open my own book to center myself. These life lessons will have to be taught over and over again. Said over and over again. Practiced over and over and over again. But never give up because our children are worth it. I am worth it. You are worth it.

My most favorite part of being a cool mom is what I call Mom Moments, those moments in life when it feels as though our hearts are about to burst inside our chests. We are ecstatic and proud of our children's actions or decisions; they are confirmation that we have made a strong, positive, long-lasting impact on our children's lives. An extraordinary Mom Moment happens when we witness our children embracing and applying these life lessons when they need strength, encouragement, patience, or resilience to overcome life's challenges. Yes, a Mom Moment indeed.

Being a cool mom is not always easy in the world we live in today. Our children are facing challenges we never even imagined possible. Cool moms will make decisions that won't always make their children happy. They will

say we are too strict, too controlling, too demanding, or too whatever. Are you nodding your head in agreement with me right at this moment? My daughters will most certainly attest to this sentiment. No matter the circumstances, cool moms stick to their convictions to raise strong, confident, self-determined, and resilient children through the arguments, tears, and hugs that follow. The only thing that matters is that our children always remember and never forget...as they travel through this journey called life...the life we have given to them...that we love them more than they will ever know, and we are with them always in heart, mind, and spirit.

Now... from one cool mom to you, a cool mom, too...the Momisms you have been waiting for...

*E*verything stems from your perspective. Your perspective influences your attitude, and your attitude influences your drive for and, ultimately, your level of success.

*K*nowledge is power. Seek it every second of every minute of every hour of every day.

"*S*omeday" is *not* on the calendar.

*S*trive to inspire people with your actions.

*E*mbrace the ordinary moments in life...they are usually the most spectacular.

*T*urn bad days into lessons learned...for tomorrow and all the days after tomorrow.

$\mathcal{N}$ever give up. Ever. When you least expect it, something great will happen.

$\mathcal{Y}$ou only get 18 magical years to be a child and the rest of your life to be an adult. Don't rush through the 9,460,800 minutes you get to be a child!

$\mathcal{A}$ moment lasts all of a second, but the memory lives forever.

$\mathcal{O}$wn your actions. Good or bad. Own them.

$\mathcal{D}$isrespect, ridicule, embarrassment, and meanness will happen.

It's how you react when they do that matters most.

$\mathcal{N}$ever underuse the words "please" and "thank you"!

11

There is no rewind button in life.

Do the right thing always. Because when you always do the right thing, you never ever have to worry about being caught for doing the wrong thing.

Do the right thing always. Even when no one is looking or will ever even know. You will know and will always remember and never forget it.

Never ever go back on the promises that you make to *yourself*. They will *always* be the most important promises you make in your life.

Too many self-imposed rules may restrict you from becoming who you want to be and more like what others want you to be.

You can't control the actions of others...only yours...and your *reaction* to theirs.

*N*othing that is happening now is permanent. Good or bad. Embrace the good times and know the bad will not be part of your future.

*C*hoices have power. Every single one.

*E*very birthday is an opportunity to start a new chapter in your life story. You know how it begins. How it ends is up to you.

*H*ow do you tell your story? Through your actions and words.

*S*urround yourself with people who inspire, motivate, encourage, and build you up to be your best.

*B*e your own sunshine even in the stormiest of circumstances.

*A*lways be teachable. In school, in sports, and in life, be teachable.

*E*veryone has their "something." Something that frustrates, something that saddens, something that irritates, and something that they wish were different. What makes the "something" different for everyone is how one deals with it or whether one simply accepts it.

You can't control what you can't control.

*H*old yourself accountable and responsible for every decision you make. Every single one.

*N*o one has or ever will be...Perfect. Don't strive for the impossible. Be proud of who you are and all your little imperfections.

*O*h, those enoughs...lose the *not* and replace with am. Am good enough, Am smart enough, Am pretty enough, Am athletic enough...Am enough, period!

*L*ove is shown, not just expressed in words.

Give what you *expect* from others. Even with the understanding that you might not get it back in return. Once in a while, you might be pleasantly surprised.

It's not a big deal that it happened, but it became a big deal when you did nothing about it.

Celebrate your *uniqueness!* It is what makes you stand out, not just fit in.

Desperation is like a three-headed monster that will make you do things you wish you had not. Always keep a tight rein on your level of desperation—whether it's to want something, to be something, or to be someone!

A famous one from Eleanor Roosevelt: "No one can make you feel inferior without your consent."

*F*eeling guilty about something you are doing is a sure sign you should not be doing it.

*A*ctions speak volumes. Make sure your actions convey who *you* are and *your* message.

*I*ntentionally build habits that build your character.

*I*f you do it right the *first time*, you won't have to worry and wonder how you will do it the second time.

*C*elebrate other people's successes... it makes you a better person.

*E*very day, every single day, holds the possibility of something amazing happening.

*S*aying "I am Sorry" is a promise...a promise *not to do* what you said "I am sorry" for again.

You are in control of your every thought and every action. Own them!

Work hard every day and never surrender to anything or anyone.

Letting go of those life's happenings that bring you sadness, disappointment, frustration, and anger is one of the most challenging things you must *force* yourself to do.

Learn from it...

Let it fuel your motivation

to think harder,

play harder, be better...

But let it go...

The impact on your life

and your future in doing so...

is immeasurable.

Discipline and self-discipline are hard to impose... but unquestionably worth the effort.

When you challenge yourself to do something different, you have already won the challenge.

Fortitude....your courage and strength during challenging times.

Don't complicate difficult situations by overthinking. Think in the simplest of terms for clarity and guidance.

Your perspective defines everything.

Challenges, setbacks, and disappointments are simply parts of life. The sooner you accept that as fact, the sooner you can plan out how to deal with them when they occur.

*T*here is no lie that is a good lie. White lies really don't exist.

*D*on't live in the past. But never forget past experiences that taught you great life lessons, either.

*B*e a person of *purpose* and *action*, not a person of complaints and excuses.

*S*ometimes the best thing that ever happened is hidden in the worst thing that ever happened.

*U*se your filter. Know...what to say...how to say it...or even whether to say it at all!

*D*on't blend in. Stand out!

*D*on't allow fear to have any say or influence on your decisions.

*E*mbrace the good, and fight through the not-so-good.

*Z*eal implies the energetic and unflagging pursuit of an aim or devotion to a cause. Let your life and dreams be the cause. Live each day with zeal!

*R*eputation vs. Character...know and understand the important distinction.

*D*on't let fear–fear of the unknown, fear of what others might think or say, fear of failing, or just plain fear–ever play a role in your decisions or keep you from going after your dreams.

*W*hen you get your feelings hurt, forgive and move on. Wallowing in your hurt feelings holds you back and doesn't fuel you to move forward.

*S*elf-pity is simply a useless waste of precious time.

*I*mpatience *rarely* triumphs.

*C*elebrate what you do well...not dwell on what you don't.

*H*ating hurts the hater...not the hated.

*C*oulda, shoulda, woulda...the three most useless words we can use. Living without regrets and what you can't change anyway is the best path forward. Learn, yes, but move on.

*W*eak mind = weak character.

*S*trive to be authentic in every aspect of your life.

*N*ever regret the decisions you make. Celebrate the great ones, yes. But make every effort not to regret the not-so-good ones. You can't change them anyway. Learn from them and *vow* not to carry your regrets into tomorrow.

*D*on't see life's problems as obstacles but as opportunities.

21

*L*augh at yourself when you make a mistake. Learn from it, yes, but be gentle.

*C*ommit random acts of kindness every chance you get. For, you see, those random acts of kindness are more *gratifying* for those who do them than who receive them.

*F*ind the inner strength to control your selfish thoughts.

*W*hen you hurt important people in your life over and over, they eventually stop allowing you to do it again.

*F*inish what you start. It may not be what you thought, hoped for, or planned. Commit to completion to build habits of perseverance and your character.

*K*ind words...use them often.

*B*e a leader, never...ever...a follower.

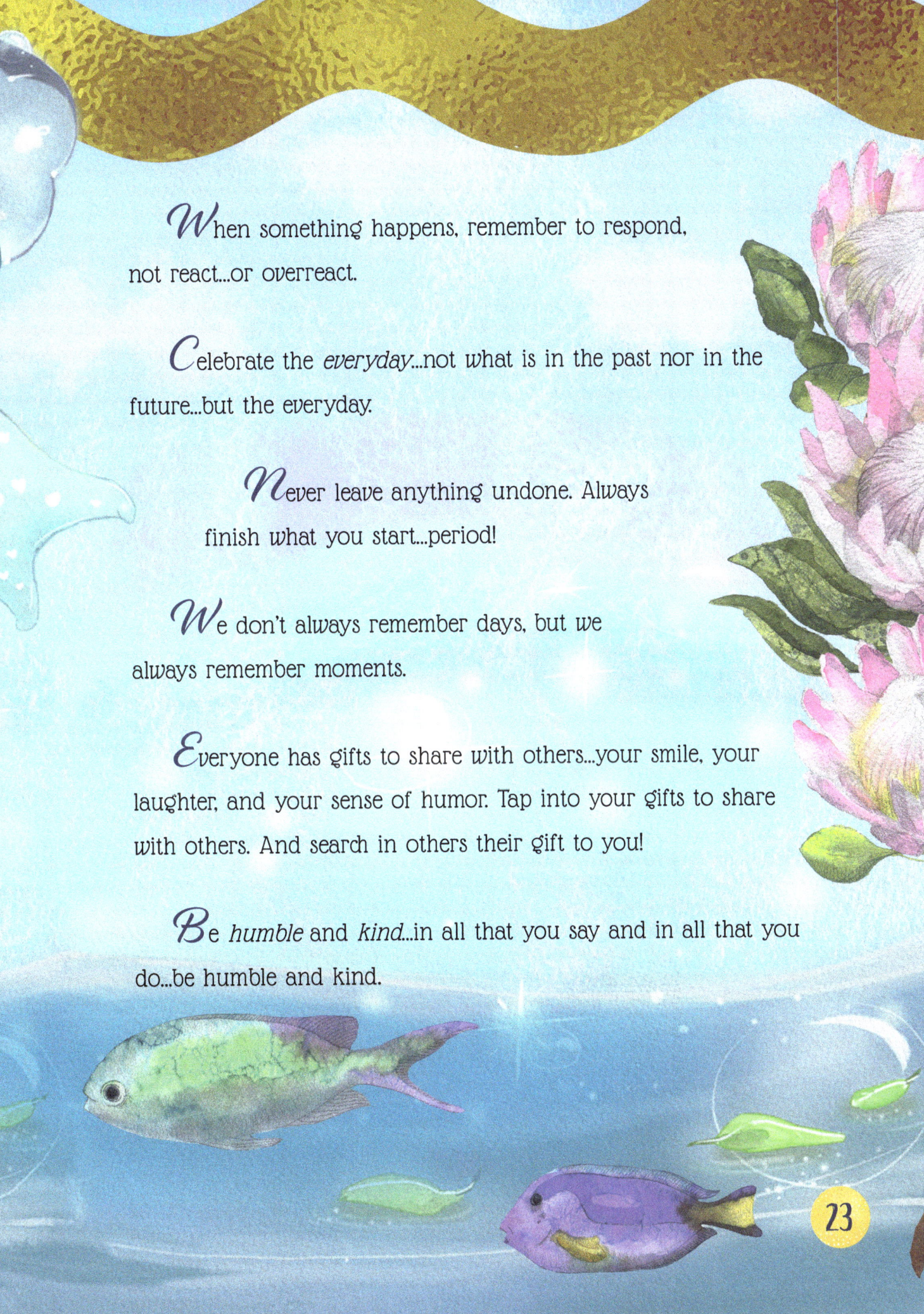

*W*hen something happens, remember to respond, not react...or overreact.

*C*elebrate the *everyday*...not what is in the past nor in the future...but the everyday.

*N*ever leave anything undone. Always finish what you start...period!

*W*e don't always remember days, but we always remember moments.

*E*veryone has gifts to share with others...your smile, your laughter, and your sense of humor. Tap into your gifts to share with others. And search in others their gift to you!

*B*e *humble* and *kind*...in all that you say and in all that you do...be humble and kind.

*U*se your words to build up, not tear down.

*A*nother superpower...accepting what you simply can't control or change.

*G*ood things always follow good people.

*C*ondition yourself not to spend time stressing. Yes, a superpower, but one worth developing.

*S*peak with clarity. Choose wisely when to use *he*, *she*, *it*, and *they*, and all those other pesky, vague pronouns, and others will clearly understand your message.

*I*s it a challenge...or an opportunity? Yep! It is all from your perspective.

*R*eflect on your past, but live in the present.

*W*ords + Actions = Character

*E*very decision matters. Every...single...one.

*H*onesty, Generosity, Patience...virtues worth developing to their fullest.

*L*ife is a continuous circle. Learn from the last loop and make the second round fabulous!

*A*lways speak to yourself with kindness.

*P*ursue your dreams. In little ways or big ways...but pursue.

*B*itterness keeps you from achieving excellence.

*N*ever expect perfection from yourself or others, and you won't ever be disappointed.

*E*njoy life's littles...they're usually biggies you remember always.

*L*ife isn't fair. Never has been. Never will be. Accept it.

*W*hen people judge you, it's more about them than you. You see, judgers don't want to be around others who will outshine them!

*T*he more we complain, the less we can see the good things we have in our lives.

*D*on't draw attention to the good deeds you do. Let them speak for themselves.

*U*se your common sense. Everyone has it. Use *yours* to its fullest potential.

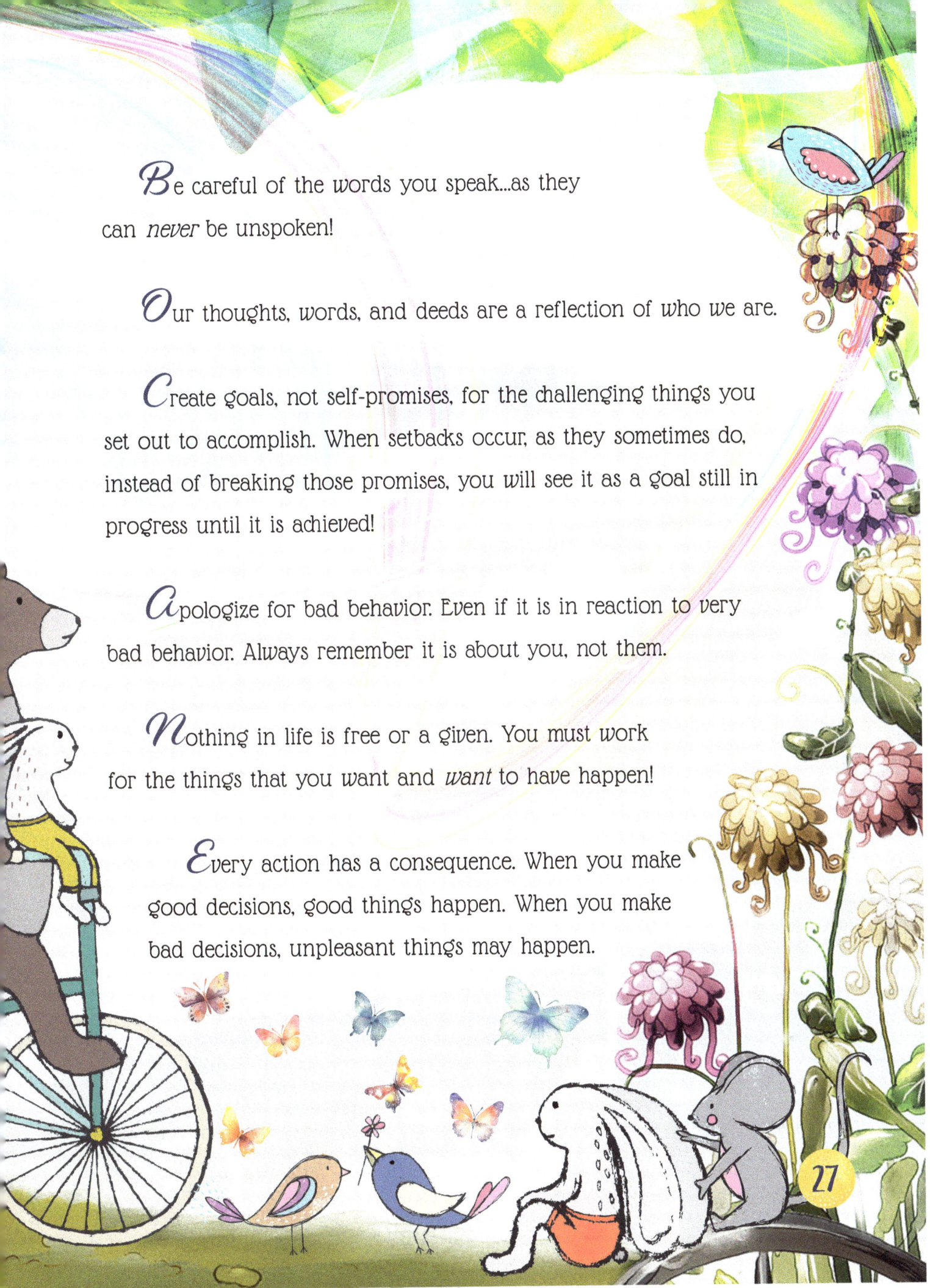

*B*e careful of the words you speak...as they can *never* be unspoken!

*O*ur thoughts, words, and deeds are a reflection of who we are.

*C*reate goals, not self-promises, for the challenging things you set out to accomplish. When setbacks occur, as they sometimes do, instead of breaking those promises, you will see it as a goal still in progress until it is achieved!

*A*pologize for bad behavior. Even if it is in reaction to very bad behavior. Always remember it is about you, not them.

*N*othing in life is free or a given. You must work for the things that you want and *want* to have happen!

*E*very action has a consequence. When you make good decisions, good things happen. When you make bad decisions, unpleasant things may happen.

*O*nly say positive things to yourself about yourself... your brain listens and remembers what you say.

*T*rying to control what you can't control wastes your time and energy. Use that energy and drive to focus on what you can control.

*T*he best thing about memories is making them. Make lots of them!

*D*on't give mean-spirited people power over you by even listening to what they say.

*B*e the person you say you are...even when no one is looking or listening.

*L*eaders lead by *example*...not by being the boss.

*I*f what you are about to say ends with "just saying," maybe it is best left unsaid.

*E*very time you point your finger at someone else in blame, three of your fingers are pointing back at you. Take responsibility for what you might have done before blaming others. It's called personal responsibility.

*Y*ou can't change the past, but you can influence your future through the actions you take today.

*N*othing ever good comes out of running a yellow light.

*C*uriosity feeds the brain. Never let it starve!

*L*ife is so much happier when you *avoid* the drama.

*B*e your own best friend.

*R*ejection...don't dwell on it. Learn from it, yes, then move on.

*L*earn to be OK with not being invited or included. Sometimes you are better for it!

*M*ake yourself proud...for you are the one who matters most.

*C*ause and effect are not just something you learned about in school. Each action you take, every word spoken or written, and every decision you make–big or small–will affect yourself and others. Always pause...and think before you act.

*C*hanging your attitude changes your perspective.

*E*njoy life's firsts. They only happen once, so *embrace* them as they happen.

*E*very day of this life is a page in *your* book.
Make it the most spectacular, thrilling book ever written!

*L*ife's little moments...make the best memories.

*S*ome thoughts should be left as thoughts
and never spoken.

*D*on't let the special moments in life pass you by
without stopping and embracing each moment.

*R*efuse to let the words of others influence what you
think of yourself....

*for sticks and stones may break my bones, but words
can never hurt me.*

31

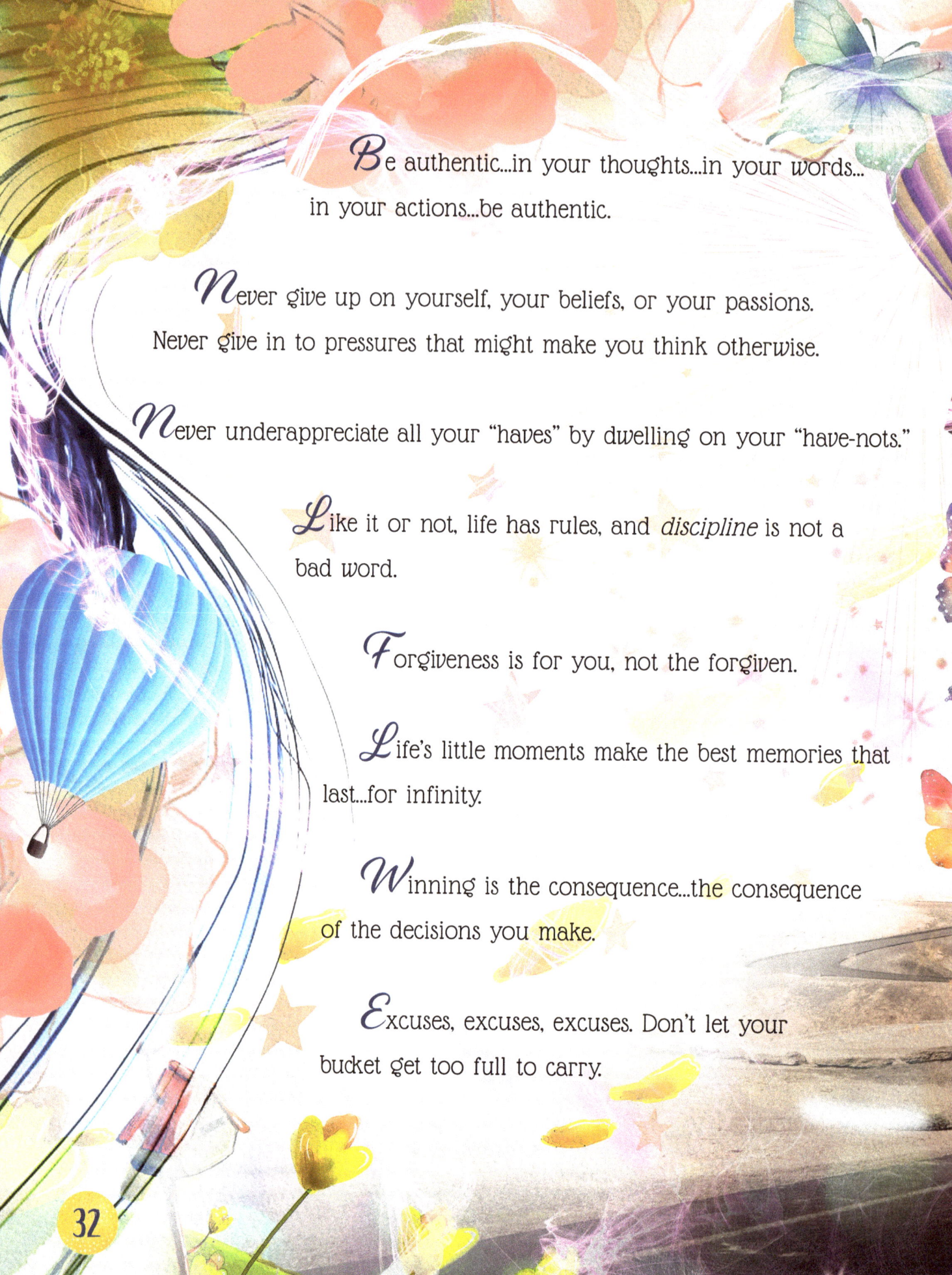

*B*e authentic...in your thoughts...in your words... in your actions...be authentic.

*N*ever give up on yourself, your beliefs, or your passions. Never give in to pressures that might make you think otherwise.

*N*ever underappreciate all your "haves" by dwelling on your "have-nots."

*L*ike it or not, life has rules, and *discipline* is not a bad word.

*F*orgiveness is for you, not the forgiven.

*L*ife's little moments make the best memories that last...for infinity.

*W*inning is the consequence...the consequence of the decisions you make.

*E*xcuses, excuses, excuses. Don't let your bucket get too full to carry.

*D*on't let the inconsideration or rudeness of others stop you from being considerate and polite. It is always about your character, not theirs.

*S*trive in all you do to *exceed* expectations, not just meet them!

*A*n oldie but a goodie...do unto others as you would have them do unto you...*even to others you know won't do the same unto you.*

*O*ne of the greatest wastes of time and energy is comparing yourself to others. Simply pointless.

*J*ust because other people break the rules and don't get caught does not give you permission to break them, too.

*A*nd lastly, always remember and never forget... *to say "I Love you" every morning and every night to those who are most important to you!*

And finally, let's return to that Impowerment app, I mentioned. Empowerment (correctly spelled with an *e*) is defined as the process of becoming stronger, more confident, and self-determined. An app is defined as a program that allows you to perform specific tasks. We have all heard or read that there is an app for just about everything we need or want. Some apps we use and depend on every second, of every hour, of every day. And some, as we have been told and might genuinely believe, we simply just can't live without. I believe that to be true—true at least for the app that I am suggesting here, and I consider it to be essential to raise strong, confident, self-determined, resilient children. But you won't find this app in any app store or be able to download it to a digital device. You see, it is not a program you install but a mindset that guides your sense of thinking, acting, and being. A mindset that drives, motivates, and fuels us to be all we can be...strong, confident, self-determined, and resilient.

Impowerment app

35

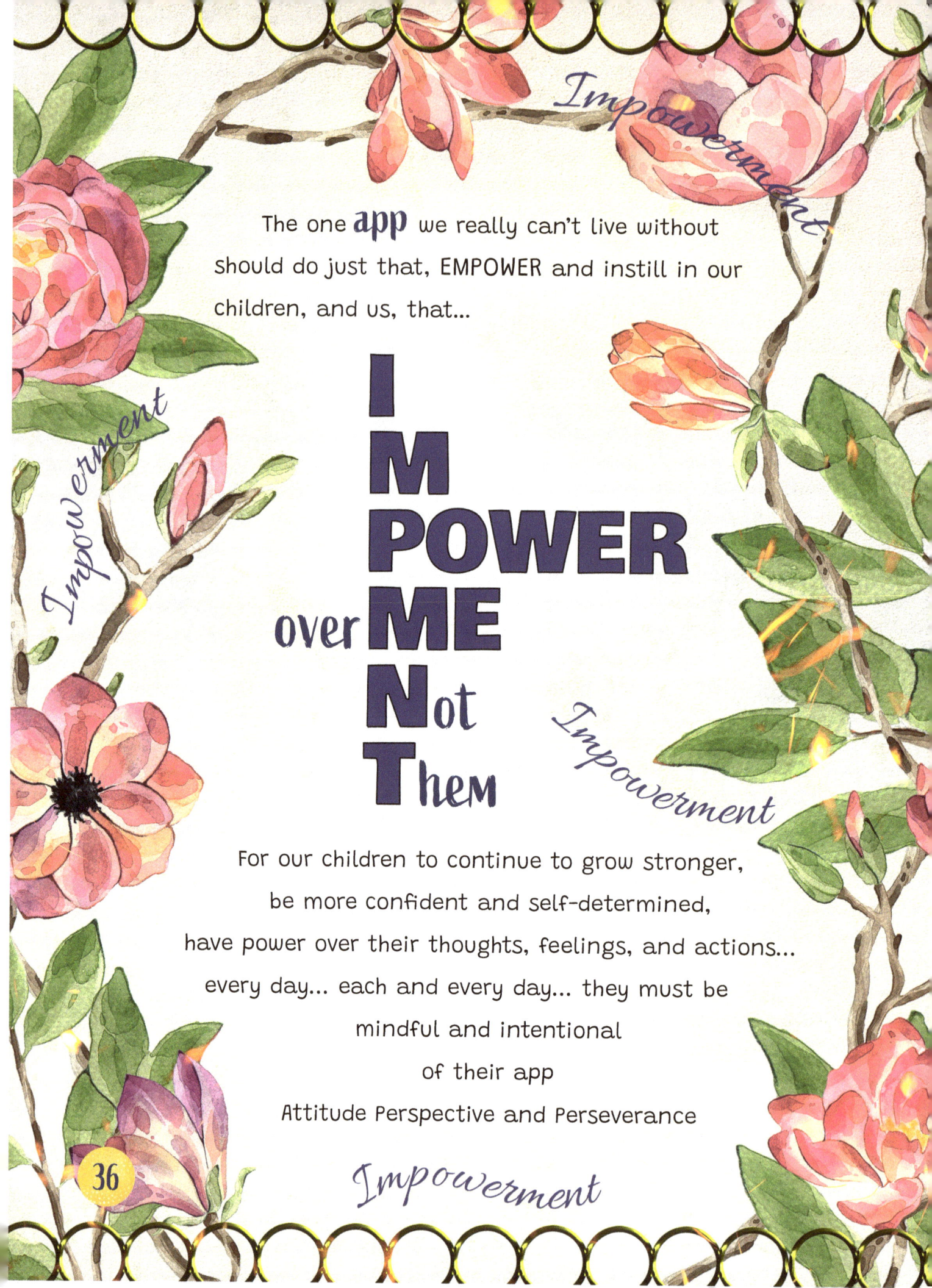

The one **app** we really can't live without should do just that, EMPOWER and instill in our children, and us, that...

I
M
over **ME**
POWER
Not
Them

For our children to continue to grow stronger,
be more confident and self-determined,
have power over their thoughts, feelings, and actions...
every day... each and every day... they must be
mindful and intentional
of their app
Attitude Perspective and Perseverance

Impowerment

your **Attitude**

Attitude

attitude—a manner of thinking, feeling, or behaving that reflects a state of mind or disposition

Perspective

your **Perspective**

perspective—an attitude toward or way of regarding something; a point of view

And ....

Perseverance

your **Perseverance**

perseverance—steady persistence in adhering to a course of action, a belief, or a purpose; steadfastness

The **IMPOWERMENT** app ignites the power to keep your

Attitude positive and optimistic

Perspective balanced and sensible

Perseverance indomitable and unflappable

Impowerment

Each and every day, if you always strive to have a positive attitude, maintain the right perspective in all that happens, and persevere through it all, you can overcome and succeed.

And just like Momisms have to be taught over and over again, said over and over again, and practiced over and over again, so is making sure the Impowerment app is rooted in your child's way of thinking and being. Don't let it be a "some days" way of thinking and being...Make it an every second, every minute, every hour of everyday way of thinking and being.

We must remind our children not to fret if their Impowerment app (Attitude...Perspective...Perseverance) is really challenged, and they don't have the energy to muster up their mental toughness, patience, resilience, or courage. They always need to remember and never forget to let one of these Momisms you have instilled in them flip that switch to kickstart their app and help them refocus on what is important. Your children may find that most days, when their Impowerment app is energized, they will be...

hAPPy and focused

stronger and confident...

and determined to accomplish whatever they dream

One final thought...I have been creating these Momisms since my daughters were toddlers. Sometimes, I just spontaneously thought of one when my child needed support, encouragement, or simply my love...to learn an undeniable truth and life lesson. Life happens in stages, and so will these Momisms. Some you can begin saying when your children are toddlers, and some you will begin saying when they start first grade. Some you will say when they don't make the sports team, and some you will say when you send your child off to college. And some, you may say to yourself daily as you journey through your own life! As you read, highlight the ones you like or modify them to create your own unique Momisms. As a Mom yourself, you probably have your own marvelous Momisms you tell your children when they need strength, encouragement, toughness, clarity, or simply love. I encourage you to write them down! Use the blank pages in the back of the book to write your own Momisms. Cool moms will do whatever it takes to keep our children confident, strong, self-determined, and resilient. All these essential Momisms, these life lessons, mine and yours, can then be passed along in our book to the next generation... and for infinity and beyond!

My Marvelous Momisms

About the Author

Children's book author Terri Peel Bechtold is the proud mother of two beautiful daughters who have been the inspiration behind all her stories, including Momisms: Life Lessons from a Cool Mom, For Infinity and Beyond, The Starfish Dance, I Am Power! Over Me, Not Them, Imperfectly Perfect (mid 2026), and I Am Enough, Period! (late 2026). Her writing is rooted in the love, lessons, and everyday moments she shares with her family—moments that have shaped her signature approach to storytelling.

Terri is also the creator of the IMPowerment App framework, a mindset built on Attitude, Perspective, and Perseverance. First introduced in Momisms: Life Lessons from a Cool Mom, this framework teaches children and adults to take power over their thoughts, feelings, actions, and reactions. Woven throughout all her books, the IMPowerment App is not a digital download, but something you activate within yourself each day—a reminder that strength, confidence, and resilience begin from within.

Terri enjoys spending time with her husband and daughters, taking adventures together, and going on long, quiet walks along the beach—her greatest source of peace and creative inspiration. She and her family reside in sunny Florida, where she loves walking, gardening, and spending time outdoors, especially at the beach.

Every day, Terri reminds her beautiful, amazing daughters—and her equally incredible husband—to always remember and never forget how deeply they are loved... every second of every minute of every hour of every day, of every week, of every month, of every year, of every decade... For Infinity and Beyond.

Terri hopes that families everywhere cherish her stories, that the messages within each book resonate deeply, and that reading them becomes a meaningful part of family traditions—especially the tradition of saying each morning and each night: Always remember and never forget... I love you... For Infinity and Beyond.